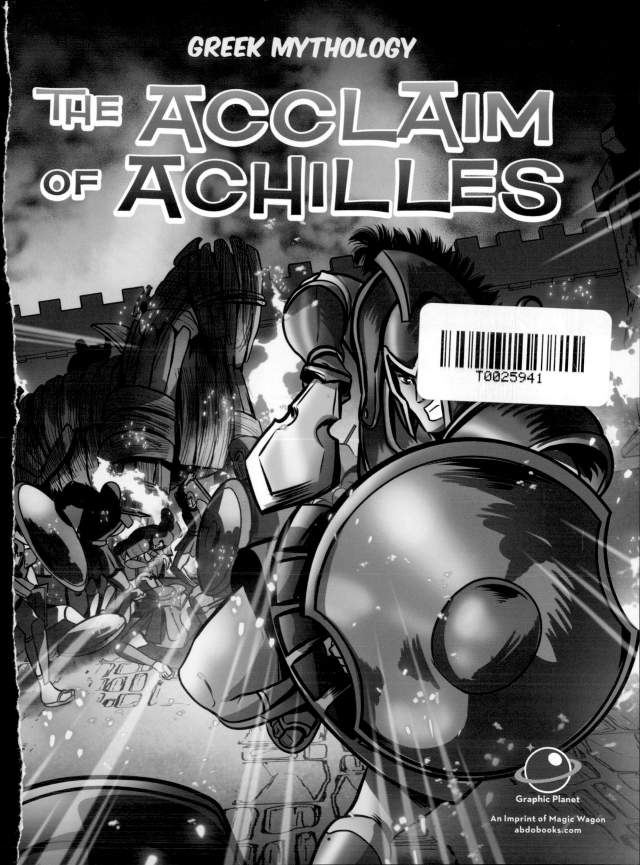

THIS BOOK IS DEDICATED TO ALL THE BRAVE MEN AND WOMEN IN THE ARMED SERVICES, WHO HAVE SERVED IN WARS NOT OF THEIR OWN MAKING. -DC

TO EVERYONE WHO LOVES A GREAT GREEK STORY ESPECIALLY MY CAT MIMITO. ILLUSTRATING THIS COLLECTION WAS CHALLENGING AND FUN. I LOVED THE WHOLE PROCESS. -LA

abdobooks.com

Published by Magic Wagon, a division of ABDO, PO Box 398166, Minneapolis, Minnesota 55439. Copyright © 2022 by Abdo Consulting Group, Inc. International copyrights reserved in all countries. No part of this book may be reproduced in any form without written permission from the publisher. Graphic Planet™ is a trademark and logo of Magic Wagon.

Printed in the United States of America, North Mankato, Minnesota.
102021
012022

THIS BOOK CONTAINS RECYCLED MATERIALS

Written by David Campiti
Illustrated and Colored by Lelo Alves
Lettered by Kathryn S. Renta
Editorial Supervision by David Campiti/MJ Macedo
Packaged by Glass House Graphics
Research Assistance by Matt Simmons
Art Directed by Candice Keimig
Editorial Support by Tamara L. Britton

Library of Congress Control Number: 2021941227

Publisher's Cataloging-in-Publication Data

Names: Campiti, David, author. | Alves, Lelo, illustrator.
Title: The acclaim of Achilles / by David Campiti ; illustrated by Lelo Alves.
Description: Minneapolis, Minnesota : Magic Wagon, 2022. | Series: Greek mythology
Summary: Achilles is brought down by his weakness in a graphic novel interpretation of this classic Greek myth.
Identifiers: ISBN 9781098231781 (lib. bdg.) | ISBN 9781644946602 (pbk.) | ISBN 9781098232344 (ebook) |
    ISBN 9781098232627 (Read-to-Me ebook)
Subjects: LCSH: Achilles (Mythological character)--Juvenile fiction. | Mythology, Greek--Juvenile fiction. | Gods,
    Greek--Juvenile fiction. | Heroes--Juvenile fiction. | Adventure stories--Juvenile fiction. | Graphic Novels--
    Juvenile fiction.
Classification: DDC 741.5--dc23

TABLE OF CONTENTS

CHARACTER GUIDE

ACHILLES
GREATEST OF GREEK WARRIORS

HERMES
TRICKSTER & FLEET MESSENGER

AGAMEMNON
KING OF KINGS

PRIAM
KING OF TROY

PARIS
SON OF KING PRIAM

HECTOR
WARRIOR PRINCE OF TROY

HELEN
QUEEN OF SPARTA

ZEUS
KING OF THE GODS

HERA
QUEEN OF OLYMPUS,
WIFE OF ZEUS

APHRODITE
GODDESS OF LOVE AND BEAUTY

ARTEMIS
GODDESS OF WISDOM AND WAR

ATHENA
GODDESS OF WISDOM

IN FACT, I OFFER A GIFT OF THE PUREST GOLD --

-- CRAFTED WITH SKILLS RIVALING HEPHAESTUS'S OWN.

IN TRUTH, THE APPLE COMES FROM THE GARDEN OF THE HESPERIDES, BUT OF THIS ERIS DOES NOT MENTION.

I HAVE COME TO PAY RESPECTS, LORD ZEUS -- OF COURSE!

TO THE MARRIED COUPLE AS WELL AS TO THESE GODS AND GODDESSES ASSEMBLED!

THIS GIFT IS IN CELEBRATION --

-- OF THE LOVELIEST THAT MOUNT OLYMPUS HAS TO OFFER.

WAIT --

-- THERE'S AN INSCRIPTION.

WHAT'S IT SAY?

INTO THE APPLE IS CARVED THE MESSAGE, "FOR THE FAIREST."

HA HA HA HA!

9

MENELAUS RETURNS TO LEARN HIS WIFE IS GONE.

WHERE IS THE QUEEN? WHO TOOK HER?

ANSWER ME!!

=GASP!=

I DO NOT KNOW, MY LORD!

THE BOY FROM TROY, YOUR MAJESTY!

SHE LEFT WITH PRINCE PARIS!

KRASSH!

MENELAUS THEN TRAVELS TO HIS BROTHER'S KINGDOM TO PLAN REVENGE.

AGAMEMNON! MY BROTHER, YOU ARE KING OF KINGS!

A SON OF KING PRIAM OF TROY HAS STOLEN MY BRIDE! IT IS TIME FOR WAR!

TROY IS NOT PART OF GREECE AND DOES NOT BEAR ME TRIBUTE.

PERHAPS DIPLOMACY BEFORE DESTRUCTION...?

"THOUGH YOU HAVE BEEN EMBARRASSED AND WRONGED, ALSO CONSIDER THAT TROY IS IMPENETRABLE.

"IT IS SAID THAT APOLLO AND POSEIDON THEMSELVES CRAFTED THE RAMPARTS THAT PROTECT THE CITY!"

AGAMEMNON'S WORDS RING WISE, BUT DIPLOMACY FAILS. HELEN DOES NOT RETURN TO HER HUSBAND.

THE SECOND PART OF THIS STORY BEGINS YEARS EARLIER, IN PHTHIA, A CITY IN THESSALY...

CRUNNCH

WAHHHH

WE NAME YOU... ACHILLES!

...WITH THE BIRTH OF THE SON OF SEA NYMPH THETIS AND PELEUS, KING OF THE MYRMIDONS.

KING PELEUS HAS ALREADY LIVED THE LIFE OF A GLORIOUS WARRIOR, SIDE BY SIDE WITH JASON AND HIS ARGONAUTS --

-- AND HERACLES IN HIS BATTLE WITH THE AMAZONS. SO HE EXPECTS NOTHING LESS FOR HIS SON.

YET THE THREE FATES, KNOWN AS THE MOIRAI, ONCE INTONED DIRE WARNINGS TO THE KING.

YOU HAVE ALREADY LOST FIVE HEIRS TO DEATH AS INFANTS.

LACHESIS

YOUR NEXT SON WILL SURVIVE AND THRIVE.

ATROPOS

CLOTHO

YET HE WILL SPILL BLOOD AND DIE AT THE HANDS OF TROJANS.

SO WITH GREAT FEAR AND GREAT LOVE FOR HER CHILD, THETIS SEEKS TO MAKE HIM IMMORTAL, IMPERVIOUS TO HARM --

-- BY SLATHERING HIM IN GODLY AMBROSIA, THEN DIPPING HIM INTO THE RIVER STYX, WHICH CONTAINS THE YEARS LEFT OF LIVES LOST.

SHOW US A WAR DANCE, PATROCLUS! CLEARLY YOUR FINEST HOUR!

I HAVE MY OWN METHODS!

YOU! FOOL!

WE SEEK KING ODYSSEUS FOR A WAR!

LISTEN, MY MEN --

-- TODAY WE GO TO WAR!!

EH? THEN ODYSSEUS WOULD BE A FOOL TO BE FOUND!

ARE YOU ODYSSEUS, THEN?

WHY DOES IT MATTER? WHAT NEWS DO YOU BRING TO MY DOOR?

ACHILLES! I RECOGNIZE YOU. KNOW THAT ALL KINGS SAVE ODYSSEUS ARE ENGAGED IN BATTLE FOR AGAMEMNON.

YOUR FATHER PELEUS IS AMONG THOSE ENGAGED IN THE SANDS OF TROY -- AND THEY ARE LOSING.

WHAT? MY FATHER IS OLD!

AGAMEMNON MUST BE MAD TO EXPECT THE INFIRM TO WAGE WAR.

I SUSPECT THE METHOD TO HIS MADNESS IS TO FORCE YOU TO FIGHT.

THEN THE KING OF KINGS HAS SUCCEEDED.

18

BY THE GODS! THIS IS NOT ACHILLES.

JUST SOME OLD MAN IN ACHILLES'S ARMOR!

WHY WOULD ANYONE ASSUME SUCH A RUSE?

FATHER -- ! AGAMEMNON BROKE HIS WORD?

WHAT TROJAN WOULD SLAY AN OLD MAN SO?

I WILL AVENGE YOU!

THE FIELD OF BATTLE IS NOT THE ONLY PLACE EMOTIONS RUN HOT AND PAINS RUNS HIGH.

I AM SO SORRY, DEAR KING PRIAM. I HAD BELIEVED MY HUSBAND WOULD MERELY FIND ANOTHER CONSORT.

I SHOULD NEVER HAVE COME HERE TO YOUR KINGDOM OF TROY. THAT HELEN OF SPARTA COULD CAUSE SUCH BLOODSHED -- !

YOU ARE HELEN OF TROY NOW, MY DEAR. MY SON PARIS'S TRUE LOVE.

WHATEVER BEFALLS MY KINGDOM, WE ALL ENDURE TOGETHER.

IN THE HOURS BEFORE DAYBREAK, SENTRIES SPOT SOME STARTLING SIGHTS.

THE GREEKS -- THEY HAVE VACATED THE SEASHORE.

THEIR SHIPS -- THEY'RE GONE! ALERT HECTOR AND THE KING!

WAIT. WHAT'S THAT BELOW??

WHAT, INDEED?

23

TROY NO LONGER STANDS. NEITHER DOES ACHILLES --

-- WHO ACHIEVES THE ACCLAIM HE CRAVES, FOR WE TALK ABOUT HIM STILL TODAY.

ODYSSEUS ENDURES, THOUGH HIS JOURNEY HOME TAKES A DECADE. BUT THAT IS ANOTHER STORY, FOR ANOTHER TIME.

GOODBYE, EVERYONE. THANK YOU FOR LISTENING.

YES, OLD MAN.

YOU HAVE A QUESTION?

I AM BLIND, SO I MAY HAVE MISSED MANY A NUANCE.

I WISH TO KNOW MUCH, MUCH MORE ABOUT THIS TALE OF TROY AND THIS HERO ODYSSEUS.

I WOULD HOPE TO WRITE A POEM OR TWO ABOUT THEM.

MY NAME IS HOMER.

I HAVE HEARD OF YOU, DEAR POET.

PARDON ME, LORD HERMES...

I HAVE READ YOUR WRITINGS.

AND WHEN WE ARE THROUGH, SO WILL MANY OTHERS!

-- END --

WHAT DO YOU THINK?

1. Prince Paris chose the goddess Aphrodite and awarded her the golden apple "for the fairest." Had he chosen Hera, what might have been the long-term result? What if he had chosen Athena?

2. King Odysseus was inspired to construct a giant horse to hide the soldiers to achieve entry into the city of Troy. Why a horse? Why do you think Odysseus believed the Trojans would bring the horse into the city?

3. Athena, Hera, and Hermes sided with the Greeks, while Aphrodite, Artemis, and Apollo sided with the Trojans. Why did each god or goddess make this choice? Why would Zeus stay out of the decision making?

4. Although Helen had many suitors for her hand in marriage, her father Tyndareus allowed King Menelaus to wed her. Tyndareus even got them to swear that they would protect King Menelaus. Why do you think her father got them to make such a promise?

5. Hermes returns time and again to roam the world, seeking the good in humanity as well as tell the tales of the many myths in which he has been involved. Why does he do this? What does he hope to accomplish? What lessons have you learned from the behaviors of the mortals and gods in this story?

MYSTERIES BEHIND the MYTHS

1. Zeus refers to Prince Paris of Troy as a fair judge. In his youth, Paris made a hobby of pitting bulls to fight against one another and offered a golden crown to any bull that could defeat his champion. Amused, the god of war Ares transformed himself into a bull and won the contest. Paris awarded the crown without a second thought.

2. In one version of the Trojan myth, Aphrodite—upon winning the beauty contest—gives to Paris her magic belt, which makes irresistible anyone who wears it. Yet no other myths refer to her magic belt or to her beauty and power coming from a magical item.

3. Did Troy truly exist? Eratosthenes, a mathematician, dated the war as 1183 BCE. In 1871, Prussian archaeologist Heinrich Schliemann began excavating a site called Hisarlik on the west coast of modern Turkey. Arrowheads, weapons, inscriptions, and signs of fire helped to confirm the location as the site of Troy.

4. Though the tales tell of a war lasting 10 years, given the true size of the city's compact location it was an exaggeration to claim the war equal the length of the Titanomachy.

5. Troy is *Troya* in Turkish and *Troia* in Latin. Its citizens were likely referred to a Troyans. Through adaptation of language through the centuries, this became Trojans.

GLOSSARY

ACHILLES — Son of the Nereid Thetis and Peleus, king of Phthia, said to be the greatest of all Greek warriors.

AGAMEMNON — "King of Kings," to whom all the regional kings gave loyalty and tribute.

APHRODITE — Goddess of love, beauty, and passion. Married to the god Hephaestus.

APOLLO — God of the sun.

ATHENA — Goddess of wisdom and war.

ERIS — Goddess of discord and despair.

GREECE — A mountainous country with many islands, located on the Mediterranean Sea. Considered the birthplace of democracy and early mathematical and scientific principles and the place from which the gods ruled.

HECTOR — Older son of King Priam and Queen Hecuba, leader of the Trojan army.

HELEN — Wife of King Menelaus of Sparta, said to be the most beautiful woman in the world.

HERA — Wife of Zeus, goddess of marriage, women, and family.

HERMES — The divine trickster, son of Zeus and Maia, the emissary and fleet messenger of the gods. He even conducted souls into the afterlife.

HOMER — Presumed author of the epic poems the *Iliad* and the *Odyssey*, about the Trojan War and Odysseus's ten-year-long journey home.

MENELAUS — King of Sparta, brother to King Agamemnon. Husband to Queen Helen of Sparta.

MOIRAI — The three Fates: Atropos, Clotho, and Lachesis.

MOUNT OLYMPUS — A real mountain in Thessaly, Greece, towering nearly 9,800 feet (2,987 m) above the sea. This is the site around which the mythology for the gods was created, with Olympia the fabled city in which the gods inhabited.

OLYMPIA — The fabled city that the gods inhabited and from which Zeus ruled, located at the top of Mount Olympus.

PATROCLUS — Soldier and friend of Achilles since childhood.

PARIS — Younger son of King Priam and Queen Hecuba.

PELEUS — King of Phthia, father to Achilles, a hero among the Argonauts.

POSEIDON — God of the sea. Son of Cronus and Rhea, brother of Zeus.

TITANOMACHY — The ten-year war fought among the Titans and the Olympians, as Zeus battled his father Cronus for control of the cosmos. Zeus's Olympians were victorious.

TROY — A walled coastal city in Asia Minor (current-day Turkey), northwest of Mount Ida, ruled by King Priam and Queen Hecuba.

ZEUS — God of lightning, son of Cronus and Rhea, husband to Hera, he fought a great and terrible war to become king of the gods of Olympus.

ONLINE RESOURCES

Booklinks
NONFICTION NETWORK
FREE! ONLINE NONFICTION RESOURCES

To learn more about **GREEK MYTHOLOGY**, visit *abdobooklinks.com* or scan this QR code. These links are routinely monitored and updated to provide the most current information available.